A Thousand
Times You
Lose Your Treasure

A Thousand
Times You
Lose Your Treasure

A Thousand
Times You
Lose Your Trea

A Thousand
Times You
Lose Your Treasure

WAVE BOOKS SEATTLE AND NEW YORK

Hoa

Nguyen

sure

A Thousand

Times You

Lose Your Treasure

Ng

Thousand

nes You

se Your Treasure

sand

ou

ur Treasure

Hoa

Nguyen

A Thousand

Times You

Hoa

Lose Your Trea

Nguyen

A Thousan

Times You

Hoa

Lose Your

Nguyen

A Thousand

Times You

Lose Your Treasure

Published by Wave Books

www.wavepoetry.com

Wave Books titles are distributed to the trade by

Consortium Book Sales and Distribution

Phone: 800-283-3572 / SAN 631-760X

Library of Congress Cataloging-in-Publication Data

Names: Nguyen, Hoa, 1967– author.

Title: A thousand times you lose your treasure / Hoa Nguyen.

Description: First Edition. | Seattle : Wave Books, [2021]

Identifiers: LCCN 2020038254 | ISBN 9781950268184 (hardcover)

ISBN 9781950268177 (paperback)

Subjects: LCGFT: Poetry.

Classification: LCC PS3614.G88 T48 2021 | DDC 811/.6—dc23

LC record available at https://lccn.loc.gov/2020038254

The author wishes to thank the Ontario Arts Council

and the Canada Council for the Arts for their grant support

without which this book would not be possible.

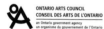 

Designed by Crisis

Printed in the United States of America

9 8 7 6 5 4 3 2

Wave Books 090

Contents

SEEDS AND CRUMBS   1

ASK ABOUT LANGUAGE AS IF IT FORGETS   2

NAMING ASSEMBLES YOU   4

"LANGUAGE POINTS"   6

AUTONOMOUS SONG   7

WE RUN ON TRASH GRASS   8

THE FLYING MOTORIST ARTIST   10

RED SHE BROKE THE CUP   13

NETTING (LANGUAGE GHOST)   14

NAPALM NOTES   17

LEARNING THE ĐÀN BẦU   18

DIỆP BEFORE COMPLETION   20

LESS THAN SLASH THREE   21

TRYOUTS FOR THE FLYING MOTORIST
ARTIST TEAM, 1958   22

GERMAN TIGHTROPE ACROBAT GROUP PAID
A VISIT TO THE VIETNAMESE HÙNG VIỆT FEMALE
FLYING MOTORIST ARTIST GROUP   24

TONES IN THE VIETNAMESE LANGUAGE   25

MUD MATRIX   26

WHY THIS HAUNTED MIDDLE AND DOOR
HUNG WITH HAUNTED GIRL BONES   28

FROM VOGUE MAGAZINE 1970   30

SING DING (GHOSTLY)   31

VIETNAM GHOST STORY: HIGH SCHOOL CLOCK TOWER   33

REVENGE POEM   35

RED SHOES GIRL SONG   37

FROM ON "NEW MUSIC" (TÂN NHẠC): NOTES
TOWARD A SOCIAL HISTORY OF VIETNAMESE
MUSIC IN THE TWENTIETH CENTURY   38

CROW PHEASANT   39

EXERCISE 14   41

OXBOW LAKE   42

MOTHER'S RIVER MOON (TRAVELING WITH THE
TRAVELING CIRCUS, LOWER MEKONG, 1959)   44

NOTES ON OPERATION HADES   45

MEXICO   47

WARM RAIN   51

FEAST OF THE FIRST MORNING OF THE FIRST DAY 52

LAST LETTER 53

DURIAN SONNET 54

DANG YOU THEN A DANG 55

UNRELATED FUTURE TENSE 57

SCOOBY-DOO VILLAIN GHOUL METHOD
A.K.A. US MILITARY PSYCHOLOGICAL
OPERATION "WANDERING SOUL" 58

HAGIOGRAPHY 59

CAN'T WRITE WHITE AND ASIAN 60

SPOKEN THROUGH THE CRACKED EYE 62

OVERSEAS VIETNAMESE 64

THỜI THẾ FRAGMENTS (CURRENT AFFAIRS) 66

OFFERINGS FOR SOULS 68

VIETNAM GHOST STORY: ĐÀ LẠT LOVERS 70

FORTUNE COOKIE NO FORTUNE 73

"O MY 4FH PLANES" (CRIES OF
JOHNSON: A FOLK OPERA) 75

TRANSPLANTS 77

SHOCK FATE | HEXAGRAM 51   79

2ND LETTER   80

SACRED FICUS SONNET   82

FAILED TOWER CA DAO   83

COLD SORE LIP RED COAT   84

VIETNAM GHOST STORY: TOWERS OF DISTRICT 5   85

SHE LEADS WITH FLOWER WANDS   86

MADE BY DOW   87

VIEWED FROM 2020   90

HEARTLESSNESS   93

WE SING TO   95

SINGS THE WISHING WELL
(THE GHOST WELL CARED-FOR)   96

HÙNG VIỆT   101

NOTES TO IMAGES   113

NOTES TO POEMS   115

ACKNOWLEDGMENTS   117

Đây là ... thời ... oanh ... liệt ... nó
năm 1956, ngày xưa em là một nữ
nghệ ... sĩ ... mô-to bay đây là kỷ niệm
duy nhất trong đời em.

   Tặng ... lưu kỷ niệm
    Anh nghệ sĩ mô-to ấy

for my mother, Diệp / Linda

A Thousand

Times You

Lose Your Treasure

A Thousand

Times You

Lose Your Tre

A Thousand

Times You

Lose Your Treasure

A Thousand

Times You

Lose Your Treasure

Times You

Lose Your Treasure

A Thousand

A Thousand

Times You

Lose Your Treasure

A Thousand

Times You

Lose Your Treasure

A Thousand

Times You

SEEDS AND CRUMBS

yes a famous mise-en-scène
"when I was just a little girl"

angle looks too much like angel
and vice versa

what lies ahead
rainbow

rainbows
who cares

scatter the song
clavichord it

the future's not ours
to see   tenderly

ASK ABOUT LANGUAGE AS IF IT FORGETS

Water glides from metal light
    lets her into life

Silver snake
somewhere-bound

A motorbike kickstand
will pierce her right knee

    take a deep piece
of meat

Fear is not part of it

(murder flies)

Let the knife thrower
nearly pierce

    her face
        not-afraid

She read the taboo novels
named daughters

for tragic rewritten heroines

trodden oceanic sorrow

She will ride ruffian

She will be the baby taken back
from her half-Khmer mother

Scars

Warm rain while naked

wistful fated
future tense

'hungry to find a good life'

NAMING ASSEMBLES YOU

She learnt
flags   penance

and ah you
not me

slow sad danced
a city street

And I packed
the jealous book   O yeah

under the highway   that is
the under-stair tailor as a

mistress seamster
  copying pants
out of *Victoria's Secret*

Bell   you called me
              bell
'captive and able'

her cuffs fancy   leaning
            with umbrellas
and dark pink feathers

    It's true

    I won't laugh again
like that   (silky)

"LANGUAGE POINTS"

from *Colloquial Vietnamese*

Word order with Thoi

With chỉ   Thoi often means "only"

He only studies
I can speak Vietnamese only a little
That's it, I will not talk anymore!

Expressing ability:

to do
to go

> I <u>can</u> speak Vietnamese.
> I am <u>able</u> to speak Vietnamese.
> I am <u>unable</u> to do it.
> I am <u>unable</u> to go.

AUTONOMOUS SONG

Refusing the motherland mother role

Delta girl plotting a runaway plot

No waiting-in-shadows life for us

Her love of colonial electric lights
    motorbikes   cursed roses   Xmas

The handsome singing
                of "Que Sera, Sera"

Barren thorns to plunge

  Bouncing light spills
   on the Butterfly Lovers
of Chinese legend

A frenzy of magenta flowers
to devour

WE RUN ON TRASH GRASS

And of course lose phone numbers   photo
of the first Hoa

burial site locations   silk
lining to sleep in   ground cinnamon

trees and coffee

Lose the word lose
in its original shape

You lose every other
word   as in most words

Now glossy
gold looks cheap   the color of loss
Joss stick & paper
smoky bundled trick &

encompassed spirit
mirrored emblem   mirrored emblem

Ghost Money

I am soot-faced as the 'feminized male god'
massive delta silt water   'Black Madonna'
Mother God
      born of thy destruction

      The running blue shock of her

THE FLYING MOTORIST ARTIST

At twelve Diệp didn't have a half cent
: entrance fee
to see the circus performance

When she was twelve
three motorcycle performers
traveled from Thailand to Cần Thơ

I thought they were
from the Philippines?
No   Thailand

A motorcycle act that came to her province
in the lower Mekong Delta
joining a country fair
for the New Year   1954

everywhere we came to see
displays of snakes
contortionists
fortune-tellers
to exchange caged birds

she the disobey

Diệp done with farm chores

   (washing clothes
       seeing to chickens
    but never the kitchen

she made things burn or break
  they said   spilled
rice in the dirt   bad luck   they said
and banned her)

    Recall that one Seer
and her mad possession: spirits in the belly
suddenly enlarged
  round and hard

When she saw the Palm Reader
       they made tell of a sailboat

  "Come see the Flying Motorist Artist!

      RIDING SHADOWS ON THE WALL OF DEATH
      RIDING SHADOWS ON THE WALL OF DEATH

Watch them defy death
on the Wall of Death!"

(danger perpendicular

their reaching hands)

Two men   a lone woman
riding
her name
loud
loud and loud

motorbike
flying

The wooden wall roars

RED SHE BROKE THE CUP

A glimpse at what is failed
exiled from heaven
to assist / those suffering /
those in peril

A bivalency and her power:

1. Snakes
2. Amphibians
3. Owl   'wh. takes night for day'
4. Bat   'half bird   half mammal'
5. Rooster who oracles the day

       etc.

Lady of the Land who laughs
a belly-centered cry

drunk from the stars
dear Lady Queen of Sky

of Forest   'hearer of the world's cries'

    as Water   clothed in white

NETTING (LANGUAGE GHOST)

You left a thread and a serious
    leather pouch   Green lined
several hauntings   yellow amber gems
to line it   left in the washroom

    Toxic mirror spit
         to whom do I speak?

As crossed and looped   a net to the wind
to meet not meeting   part

Purple covers me in lips   hand like a branch-hand
   Tree bound
Chased into trees

If the mind says button-on-the-cuff

If the mind doesn't mind this reaching
    into your pocket and pulling out the lining
      cut it out completely

xxxxxxxx and xxxxxxxx

for the Languageless

Girl (chewing ice)

Face turned blue then purple

later crooked bangs of straw

I was the no-name garbage can

new teeth bit

and lost lid

I get things wrong like this

New shoots to shoot through

This not-enough-ness

learns me to be Tough

bitten web of thumb

we call confidence

lost most tones

and a young woman named Five

who cried

Nowhere

Nowhere

Say "Happy Birthday"

Cut out eyeholes to see

NAPALM NOTES

Developed in secret
at Harvard   produced

by Dow Chemical
An efficient incendiary formula

perfected on Valentine's Day
1942   A thickened

gasoline   Can be
dropped from planes

(napalm bombs)
also flamethrowers

8 million tons of bombs
in Vietnam   Burns at

1,500–2,200°F   (1/5th as hot
as the surface of the sun)

Very sticky   stable
also   relatively cheap

LEARNING THE ĐÀN BẦU

The monochord of Vietnam
typically used for lamenting songs
traditionally sung by blind players

Single string with resonator
(empty coconut shell)
manipulated by a stick
plucked entirely in harmonics

Also called
'gourd zither'

Pluck it with some kind of pick
the notes are clear and bell-like
Fairylike   a winged string

Flexing the string
the pitch rises and falls
the notes 'trill'

It sounds like the Vietnamese voice
they say

the pitch bending the way
the voice holds sway
bends towards the Vietnamese voice

old as war   old as epic

A poor person's instrument

With an electric pickup and amp
you can make it sing

Welcome to the Hotel California

DIỆP BEFORE COMPLETION

Her first name
deemed too delicate
for a failing baby

    She was a baby failing
(arrived blue   feetfirst)

Newly named Diệp after the strapping
Chinese butcher

Renamed   she recovers!

    She says later
"It's an ugly sounding name"
and thus not popular

I say it wrongly
fake my way

Do we believe in
the Compassionate Protector
        of Children?

The past tense of sing is not singed

LESS THAN SLASH THREE

I feared I would lose it
taking a running leap at the song

the design half horsefly half dragon-
fly   Vietnamese valour rising up

of an otherworld journey I took
reclined on a couch on Horse Bridle Trail

Yes radiant string speak for me
I become a voice   Elemental

lame-foot herb-knowing healer
I met   He the locally feared mage seer

(It was a quest for understanding)
We both laughed when I quoted

Rilke in English equating beauty
with terror   the way my mother

was *not* impressed when I sang
my rendition of "It's the Hard Knock

Life" for us

TRYOUTS FOR THE FLYING
MOTORIST ARTIST TEAM, 1958

She tried   sliding
pedaled torn pants

Tryouts
a "test of strength"
in the Barrel   Ride a bicycle

Are you sure : a bicycle?

A bicycle

Push and pedal
Climb high banked sides

to try again and fall
to try again
and fall

(running blood)

They said: ok, stop,
enough, you're in!

22

She said   "I was the darkest one
    and the prettiest"

To 'save' performance shoes   they trained barefoot

    She took a taste of earth
held hands on the Wall of Death

GERMAN TIGHTROPE ACROBAT GROUP PAID A VISIT TO THE VIETNAMESE HÙNG VIỆT FEMALE FLYING MOTORIST ARTIST GROUP

On Friday night, 21-1-1960, at 22h30, the ZUGSPITZ ARTISTEN aerial tightrope acrobat group went all the way to Xóm Củi to pay a visit to the Vietnamese Hùng Việt Flying Motorist Artist Group, comprised of young women aged from 16 to 21 years old.

On this occasion, Madam Huỳnh Thị Kết, the director of the Hùng Việt Female Flying Motorist Artist Group held a reception to welcome the foreign artists. The German artists highly praised the Vietnamese female flying motorist artist group because according to them, in Germany and in Europe, only men could perform as flying motorists, and rarely women. The German artists think that if the Hùng Việt Flying Motorist Artist Group is allowed to travel overseas, their performances would be warmly received and enjoyed by audiences abroad.

TONES IN THE VIETNAMESE LANGUAGE

Ma—level : ghost

Má—high rising : mother

Mà—low falling : but

Ma.—low constricted : rice seedling

Mã—dipping rising : horse

Ma?—low dipping : tomb

MUD MATRIX

Drown vs flood
    Silken mud
Burned burrowing creature
with strong rodent teeth

Mekong moon story
    write water on water

 Write country

    Float on flat boats
   river moon   reflective
and her voice there

She is shrugged now
 high collar   quality TV channel
brassy

what electric ribbon of water
re-
    becomes delta
        fish and moving mouths
as the nine dragons move more

Grateful bastard
  the passport
proud   amoeba thin
      comes with knees
  a scratchy please
            of refugee

Ching   a cartoon plunder
Chong   a gangplank gratitude

  we the
expected happy   thankful pleasing
thankful pleasing

//// one broken jade bracelet ////

    Mother gone to mud
How to hook her
  and stop her flying hair

Can eat a tooth or other
crumbles
    bird beak tooth

No it's flies in your eyes

WHY THIS HAUNTED MIDDLE AND DOOR
HUNG WITH HAUNTED GIRL BONES

Yellow and pink comforter ending in pom-pom
fringe on Flanders Avenue   She'll die

here by choice   ashes in the backyard
not in a circular cement bomb shelter for one

Go into your tree   roll on a rabbit fur blanket
refuse to eat for thirty days   plus ten days

    Unremembered   does it matter
misremembering the baby she lost   a different baby

(unborn   never born   the unnamed)
    This rain reminds me of rain

I cleaned the pain but smell it on floorboards
of a Ford Fiesta   maybe need to burn effigies

powder puff   French cosmetics
and perfumes   the tortoiseshell hairbrush father

gave her in Saigon   "My Butterfly"   he wrote

in the long lost   This is a clichéd test

stuff the alarm clock   in my bag   Clouds

and black in the afternoon   (untranslatable)

This is the year of the orient—of the Shanghai Express, the kimono, the obi belt, the lotus flower, the Korean rice picker, the crackles in ancient celadon vases, the murals of Tunhwang, the K'ang Hsi porcelain, the sang de boeuf, the Manchurian white forehead, the Island-of-Yezo green, the Japanese clogs, the coolie hat, the enamel butterflies, the capes—all of which appeal to our fantasy in search of the lost paradise . . .

SING DING (GHOSTLY)

Where is she buried   the first Hoa
gone to ground (buried
        in Mekong mud)
dead unknown years
        drowned in lung matter

The first Hoa had not medicine
            I got it
    (the medicine)

    and got the golden visa
    and the ash hair
and breathings
lashings to a raft life
lashed to life   the blonde
        joke of
    pull eyes

    Mother swims from the nest
pushes sand first   scrapes flat flipper feet
\\\We come from egg and make it

        are the lived-loved thing

cracked leather egg from dragon-fairy mating

left warm in warm sand

        She

buried the nest us   as nest   so we could unbury

gulp sand

   Few kin in the sand

           we seek under

beached beach   moon beach   the moon-water beach

This isn't doing anything like redemption

Dodad   Mountain Dragon   unsuffering

did slither to seaways

Who are you who talk tits and knee shame

Sing ding-dong songs at me   Boys

I called it unsufferable   said

I'll meet her in heaven where the perfume is

I say I'll meet you

there   Hoa

VIETNAM GHOST STORY:
HIGH SCHOOL CLOCK TOWER

The cursed object in the high school
is a clock tower

The curse arose from a secret teenaged
love story and a pregnancy
discovered by the families
with many objections
and keeping them apart

The clock tower is the site
of her pregnant suicide

    and now the room
inside the tower is kept locked

Mist surrounds the room

A purple áo dài ghost haunts the hallways
A purple áo dài phantom
    wanders the courtyard
        sits under a banyan tree

Sometimes the high school principal
places magical amulets
& burns offerings
inside the room   to appease
the purple áo dài ghost

and that seems to help
somewhat

REVENGE POEM

Spoiler alert: she drowns and turns

into a bird   I turn into my mother

with my cruel quip and absent father

    nest 7, 11, or 14 days

The sea loves me as I calm her

her and her withered left side

an opioid song she sings taking C

for a very large cookie and I truly

am the horrible-ist wanting

    the oracle to tell me first

        to expect the drowning sea

Come lap lap lap back

  lap another way back

 sags

Skully sag-faced   Why build the nest

on the sea when your name means

scree   serene

know why the ease time

These are my radiant fur scars
my fur scarf and trinket necklace
with the long brass (tarnished)
chain

Chem-sprayed burn scar
"Strawberries," he said

RED SHOES GIRL SONG

How many wives
How many sacks
How many cats
How many kits
How many life

blue for a face   blended in place
and a cutie bastard
cutie bastard   bag of chips

The red shoes she wore
        were vain-in-the-church
The dancing   I met there   A man

He had objects
He had objects
He had objects   exponentially

Her knee-skinned velvet
Her broken fleeing / a kind of moon

Her doom was nonacceptance

FROM ON "NEW MUSIC" (TÂN NHẠC): NOTES TOWARD A SOCIAL HISTORY OF VIETNAMESE MUSIC IN THE TWENTIETH CENTURY

Thematically, the three most common types of songs in *tân nhạc* are

(1) songs that express a cosmic yearning for a homeland that is tragically inaccessible,

(2) songs that express a cosmic yearning for a love relationship that is tragically inaccessible,

(3) songs that express a cosmic yearning for a beautiful time in the past that is tragically inaccessible.

Vietnamese listeners, one sometimes feels, are never totally content until their music is totally tragic.

CROW PHEASANT

You can wave off the gnat or join it
in the next life   live two hours

   plus three days or 800 years like an 800-
year-old banyan tree   beat the drums of spring
                     for the near-me new moon

I kick the wicker dog   kick it
   hard to explain the ancient joke

How to be vast and slow compassion

   The strange girl
you named High-up-in-the-pond-sky

         But you didn't know how to spell "reckon"
very well   You misspelled reckon   and hooked me
                   into a graffiti of surrender

   Grow old bones to eat pain

Fuck-off renewal candle and burn the metaphor

Despite claims of no birds in Vietnam
(because of our constant eating aggression)

who wants to hear
about your Asian North American experience anyway

if I write flowery and incomplete

We bird you to the sky   and suffering released there
We cry city mountains

I came to
tame with a song bowl
a sung swap to dynamite
the arthritic as an
expansion trick

A true jade vibration travels as it sounds
sending a vibration up the face
pyramid-shaped

She was born "in a halo"

Delta mouth begins the sentence

coop coop coop call of pheasant crow

EXERCISE 14

from *Colloquial Vietnamese*

Translate into Vietnamese.

Are you happy, Miss?

Why are you so sad?

What have you come here for?

Are you English or American?

Are you a tourist or a businessman?

Are you a diplomat or a tourist?

What did you do during the war?

Were you an American military officer during the war in Vietnam?

Why do you ask such a question?

OXBOW LAKE

I might forget the long slow
buildup and cornball delivery of HBD
the remix   sung years old
    answering machine
  makeup dust
  and compacts I threw out
the whole makeup tote bag half-used blush
pencils and what else
  a curse inside nautilus

   the hard final years were hard years going
blind no going outside
or hardly and then to doctors
  bebop de bebop boom radio
of the sketchy pastoral on romance-y
bolster covered in American toile

  and in her handwriting
  the notebook full of figures
"Jonathan $200" etc
   and that one that said
  "My Treasures"

orpheus butterflies   ebony jewelwing

how much cloudface rainbow rage
busting out saying "Silly Girl"

   my favourite lake
 being the orphaned one   made
when the meandering became too strong
I forgot to sniff kiss the children
 now they've grown

MOTHER'S RIVER MOON (TRAVELING WITH THE TRAVELING CIRCUS, LOWER MEKONG, 1959)

            Sways   laughing
            to glint past
          river river
        and
          river-parted lovers
        of myth
          : \\\\\ ///// :

        a story of brushing hair

        River full moon
          glows
        low

            follows

NOTES ON OPERATION HADES

Renamed: Trail Dust
Code name: Operation Ranch Hand
Call sign: Hades

1961 to 1971
Approximately 20 million gallons or
an average of 5,355 gallons per day
for 3,735 days

"Rainbow Herbicides"

Agent Pink (testing stages)
Agent White (2nd most used)
Agent Green (green stripe on barrel)
Agent Orange (most widely)
Agent Purple (similar to Orange)
Agent Blue (crop destruction)

Applied aerially
dense coastline sprayed from boats

Mixed with jet fuel (diesel)

Monsanto Corporation
Dow Chemical

MEXICO

Opening a fruit stand after
her time in the circus
   more exactly could you say
   a juice stand?

Refreshments by water
   Vĩnh Long province
to arrive by boat or foot
     for a fresh drink
to drink by the river made
and served by her or her friend
also formerly of the circus
together they opened a little stand
by the water as a business
1964

     In the beginning
just setting up really   sorting out
what kinds of juice? Plain and mixes
papaya   dragon fruit   some ginger in there
things I don't know the name for
   coconut   you name it

A handsome captain came by
    tall   strong
cheek-boned face
    Minh was his name
              asked the name
             of this place

      What was she to name it?

She hadn't thought of one yet   she admitted

  Minh had just returned
    from military training abroad
had returned from Mexico
where he had been sent
   to train

  His brother also a captain
trained in Mexico too and he knew
how to steer that one complicated
   military boat in Saigon

        Mexico
he suggested
   You should call it "Mexico"

,,,·····\\\\\,,,,,·····

She named her stand Mexico

    and Minh came by often
would send his soldiers there
   to buy drinks
from her Mexico

   Mexico became the most popular
juice spot on the river

     but sometimes his soldiers were
boisterous and caused trouble   other
merchants were jealous
of her success   Minh too
wished to control her
   insisted later that she move
away from her Mexico to Saigon
       to be near him
         and next was that

How old was she?   Early 20s
after her sweet Hoa died

she became pregnant by Minh
who was married and yet wanted her with him
and when she gave birth to a son

who arrived finely shaped and "very long"

He would grow tall
she thought

she gave the son to Minh's
wife   and then she was free   and didn't see
  him again

WARM RAIN

rain is a blessing from god she said

covered in hose water and mud

washed out washington dc stars

night sky   exit window to low roof

thousand-miles-away wall scene

hand-painted on rice paper

she knew her worth

the halo born

Buddha blest she was

precipitation (n.)   "act or fact of falling headlong"

FEAST OF THE FIRST MORNING OF THE FIRST DAY

You want money to flow into the house like water
and leave the house like a turtle

No sweeping or cutting on Tet
Don't sweep or cut your luck

Earth cakes are square
Eat them

The Kitchen God rides the carp

Wear your best new outfit
Invite a rich neighbor through the door

Yellow apricot flowers bloom
tied with red ribbons

Burn incense for the ancestors
Hang poems on the walls

LAST LETTER

17 March 73

Dear Sister

I want you to know that the money you sent $100 to my mother I couldn't/hadn't been able to withdraw from the bank at the bank they said they had to check with the bank in the US to make sure that the amount has been transferred to such a person and that it is available in the account so right now all that my mother has in the bank is a receipt that she should come back in a month to Saigon to withdraw the money but I'm not sure how much she will be able to get

I received the letter and photographs and gave the letter to Cô Út

In two days it will be the anniversary of my father's passing away and so I'm letting you know this so you won't be expecting a letter anytime soon and I'll tell you about the money and how much the bank gave us in the meanwhile I hope that everyone is happy healthy and that the children are growing up steadily and are nice kids and that you will always be this beautiful lady

we are concerned and in good health
talk to you later in another letter

[unsigned]

DURIAN SONNET

I lost this sonnet once   I may lose it again
I wore the design described as concealment
and surprise   The split sides and hugged features
You had to lift your arms out for the poster

photograph   You had to leave your arms out
to show your Circus Daring   to say you chose this
To say you are flying   flying   fucking flying
on the small French motorbike   Hair

also flying and a glamour shot smile   I ask Diệp to tell
me who they are   the women pictured in black & white
colourful stripes   5 in the all-women motorcycle troupe
(Durian translates as "private sorrow")   She says

Hm, I think she's dead   I don't know what happened to her
She killed herself   I don't know what happened to her

DANG YOU THEN A DANG

trip me up
a startled robbed way

dreamt a burnt stump
for a tongue

Ash-haired girl
   Cowbell girl

the white American
Veteran said   Children

like you played
in the garbage

(leftovers)

She said 'I left my ease here'
   heavy trays   trick knee

the trick of the model
   minority   (a favoured

shitty condition)
We rung up the diction-tones

to be proud   we were
  'I threw you away'

and old skins shed
  as a Silver Snake (1941)

  sweet toddler on the
crook of her hip

UNRELATED FUTURE TENSE

with me being a bastard
and Saigon tea   will ask about my language
people will ask about bar girls
even without food in the poems
they will smell fish sauce and phở
ask about 'the war' which is to say
about men fathers and soldiers
about white Americans what
about them
about them
about white Americans what
about men fathers and soldiers
ask about 'the war' which is to say
they will smell fish sauce and phở
even without food in the poems
people will ask about bar girls
and Saigon tea   will ask about my language
with me being a bastard

SCOOBY-DOO VILLAIN GHOUL METHOD
A.K.A. US MILITARY PSYCHOLOGICAL
OPERATION "WANDERING SOUL"

[. . . Enter Buddhist Funeral Music . . .]

Who is that? Who is calling
me?   My daughter? My
wife?

. . . .

My body is gone   I am dead
                    my family!

. . . .

It was a senseless death

How   How
senseless   senseless

Go home   go home my friend
before it is too late!

HAGIOGRAPHY

A saint she ain't

CAN'T WRITE WHITE AND ASIAN

(rice)
　　also associated w/
fish and life　　vehicle for sauce

not the Xmas bombings known as
"12 Days of Darkness"

which like the lesser-known (?)
　　1945 "Great Hunger"
are Northern
　　　　colonial catastrophes

Here be chopped things

　　Infused identity
Anise star　　or pepper it

no daughter in this lifetime
　　suffice it to say　as they say

Clear the eyes
    with chrysanthemum

and how do you protest disaster?

'You are lost and gone forever'

SPOKEN THROUGH THE CRACKED EYE

Drink from the stars
womb-woven song

silt-sift
    silt gift
slit mouth spilled open
        and grain pours out

to be free and alive

arms out like wings on either side

You'll stab each other like needles
    said her grandfather
        with his star charts
and too many books for a farmer

but what
about the aborted 'babies'

Of course
their souls fly and help us in counsel

can cauterize memory

But what
happens   when luck happens
her solo memento
that photo

an island delta root nest
a dragon tongue drum
and leatherette clasp purse

"In the future even stones will need each other"

OVERSEAS VIETNAMESE

Now I trail myself
   the main travelway
This is a journey oblong

upper-body movement moving me
toward the cartoon
   version of movement

We press toward
the massacre tower

   The sniper tower
I once designed tours for

///

She told me her memory ghost
dreams
  deep-set
  embroidered vines

 a long-haired girl
 inset mother-of-pearl

Venus w/ fingernail
new moon

We ask about spent flowers We ask no-
    things unanswered red garnets

birthed and hollowed out

    A box of rose
        but also not rose

Born of thee who dies more

(now I trail myself)

      She put her pain there
brass planter bougainvillea
    glossy lacquer

She will die ordinary
    rehearse the story

we be   we
transcend history

THỜI THẾ FRAGMENTS (CURRENT AFFAIRS)

Monday, June 19, 1967: torn and folded newspaper scrap

Headline: plane crash survivors in Bảo Lộc
"Horrific 24 hours in the deep jungle"

Bài Học Anh Ngữ
"English Lesson": tune in at such & such time
to follow along on such & such radio frequency

Solar and Lunar calendars: not a good time for praying,
opening a store, holding a wedding. Auspicious: meet friends,
enrol in school.

Here are the lucky ages
Here are the lucky numbers

"Darkness of Đồng Pha Lan"
Spy novel featuring the characters Phượng & Mr. Quỳnh;
installment #19.

Local affairs:
>   Rules about elections
>   The importance of rural development

Issues faced by manual workers in ports
and drivers of xe lam (three-wheel trucks)

International oil business, the Arab-Israeli conflict, Iran, Suez Canal
re: supply / production

"Newsmen were barred from *government-industry talks* (16)"

OFFERINGS FOR SOULS

Festival Day of Lost Souls   or

Forgiveness for Lost Souls Day   or

Forgive the Lost Souls Day   or

Wandering Souls Day   or

Feast for Wandering Souls   in

the "month of lonely spirits":

1. Food (arrayed)

2. Hell banknotes (burned)

3. Symbolic objects (burned)

4. Other gifts (burned)

5. Votive gold paper (burned)

One must release captive birds

also fish

    Food offerings at the end of the day:

                given to the poor

         & the children

VIETNAM GHOST STORY: ĐÀ LẠT LOVERS

A student at the military school   1956
and a literary teacher at the nearby high school
fall in love   Cute:

each day after school the military student left
a love letter on her door   Thao (an orphan)
wrote back and left a love letter reply on the door
        of her small house on the hill

Their love grew like a stack of letters

    They were in love and waited
for Thahn to graduate from military school
            before living as a couple   officially

Unlike Thao   Thahn is from wealth
            and his rich parents insist that
upon graduation   he return home
to the Delta   and marry a local girl of their choosing

            Unable to defy them   he does

Thao   devastated   jumps into a lake
drowns   leaves a letter
with instructions to bury her body
near her house and the memories
of her love for Thahn
        on the love letter hill

Thahn finds out about her death
        goes to war   is killed
and then buried in Đà Lạt
next to his beloved Thao
    on the hill   per his written wishes

But
the widow   spurned in death
won't leave it at this

    She instructs that his body be removed
and taken back home to the Delta

    What a terrible
        idea

and now his ghost wanders

Actually
both sites are haunted by their ghosts

and Đà Lạt made the site on the hill
into an attraction you can visit
because why not

FORTUNE COOKIE NO FORTUNE

not quite meandering chi luck
more like vermillion songbirds than orange
  figure
maybe nine months postpartum

a Kodachrome print
in a 'standard' squarish size
  a size no longer a size

a floating island

she learned English from *The Young*
 and the Restless   a basement waterfall
lights up   leaning

clay-colored flowerpots we grew in

the way she sewed
    language silent months

back then in Vietnam
"a mixed child was as good as dead"

remember the small wrapped cakes?

they open to see a flower

wet eyelashes

"O MY 4FH PLANES" (CRIES OF JOHNSON: A FOLK OPERA)

Born Phantoms
we have become phantoms

o you powerful Thunder Chief
God of Thunder himself
thunderstruck

o crusaders   o flying sabres
o sky raiders
o sky runners
you have returned to the sky

o US Air Force
if the Gods love you
find your way back
to America!

Thus cries our poor Johnson
and we tell him:

"Pirates always receive
the deserved punishment
the deserved punishment

Enraged you still bite
like an unrelenting blind player

If you have any spirit left
go back home
back home!
go back home!"

TRANSPLANTS

so we are poor people
   transplants
halfway round the planet
photographs
  destroyed or hid
     from 'authorities'

who am I to you   Statue
who shimmers like history

what happens when fate happens

     what 'fate'

hand-painted lacquered kitten heels

  we had abortions
she won't let you record

a boat crossing water
  propelled by
long crossed paddles

and no I don't want to conduct
Mỹ Lai research and produce it
for you here
    Dear Reader

  here we see a different metal
guns pointed from a decommissioned
cannon

  on the farm her aunt returned from paddies
to nurse the baby

milk soaks her shirt

  we won't be rescued
by self-serving benevolence &
  holy books

      lost-looking woman
who cries and wanders

the common trauma aftermath
    of any person   walking and crying

    yes   I hate this
poem too

SHOCK FATE | HEXAGRAM 51

She mistook the munitions blasts for fireworks

She said goodbye to her lover

She threw the photographs into the canal

She dressed as an "old woman"

She shaved my head (my hair too light from the white father)

She took off her jewelry

She took in neighbors   but not by choice

She could have been labeled "a counterrevolutionary"

       and dumped into a mass grave

She could have said that I wasn't her baby

Vĩnh Long, Tet 1968

2ND LETTER

17 March 73

[More difficult to decipher, unsigned]

I just received your letter . . . I wanted you to know that MyLy is a very good kid and the younger one I've heard that she is very cute and that you are all in good health. I hope that you have what you will. I wish you a hundred years of happiness to you and the children. Here my mother and my sisters are all OK. Cô Út is as usual and the boy is going to be drafted soon unless my mother has 30K dong to give [as a bribe] to stay at the village and he doesn't have to go to the army. If you can help her with the money bc she doesn't know where to turn to find that money . . . bc we are poor and also next February [how is this possible? the letter was written in March—she might mean the 2nd month of lunar year] we have a ceremony to organize for the passing away anniversary and we are going to need 10K bc this time I want to do a big event bc I want to invite ppl that supported my mother when my father passed away otherwise my mother wouldn't do anything grand bc we are poor and 10K dong is a lot of money and in our situation it is impossible to borrow 10K dong esp. when you know that you have to reimburse 12K.

There will be a change of address if in your next letter please write the new address Cần Thơ . . . I hope you will send my mother some money for the ceremony for the death anniversary so that they don't have to borrow from a third party.

SACRED FICUS SONNET

Cinched belt tugged tight around the heart
5 or 6 aerial roots dangling   A strangler fig

Do homeless ancestors live inside the tree?
Child of noise   Hold the loosened ends   You

may miss the moon or fall in love with it   Embrace
ashes   I too am far removed   A thirst that wanders

thirsting   And I could never ask the name of the boy
who died   A baby boy who died but what could you do

and maybe words hang in sinew and care   Writer
of dead words or living words and life's hammer

Encase the host tree and erase it   I don't know
the folk songs on farms far from here   The dead buried

and gone   To dig the grave   Who dug the graves
Darling   the sea widens for you tonight   and deepens

FAILED TOWER CA DAO

sonnet tied to the sky
struck by lightning
in that one film version
of Frankenstein who
was it that feared
the storm and lightning

myth and history twist
exile into a tower structure
also called "mouth"
that feeling of headlong
the site of mother
my longing in language

see my eyes rubies red   I feed
on toxic flowers   kiss one
or any flower   rise clean from
mud water   row a petal boat
absurd longing to sing the sun
to exist and live an island of

COLD SORE LIP RED COAT

What if I ate too much food   there being
not enough money   immigranty
and save all the ketchup
                        packets   George
Carlin record on the record player
of how many ways to curse   and they
are all funny

   (small brown bird with a black
neck and a beak full of fluff for a nest)

    The old joke: "How many feet
do you have?"   instead of
"How tall are you?"

This looks like joy   a joke
who looked at you and laughed

Look at the map upside down   so that south
is north and north is south
        it's the other
way around because it's the commonly agreed to
thing   (visual language of the colonizer) or
snowful awful   tearful wishful

VIETNAM GHOST STORY: TOWERS OF DISTRICT 5

Formerly pink towers
 now green

Maybe the entire complex is haunted
a single light lit in a complex of windows

Deaths   a suicide   or several   (women)

Remodeled with fresh green paint
it is renewed
 serves as a business complex
  features a McDonald's

SHE LEADS WITH FLOWER WANDS

Made by the dead puppeteer the rings
found them it seemed   Dry papery magenta

flowers of the wild bougainvillea

Multiple ghosts jab your throat   thorns
in the uninterrupted kitchen dream

They could see it was perfect so their prophecy

was fulfilled   so the lung smothered dies
so they wrote down their dreams

Their way made unpassable so fall through

worlds   dashing the red gourd
                    of light on the way

MADE BY DOW

The white woman   rather thin with a cinched
vintage coat who I met and later referred to as 'Pillbox'
(saying 'I call her Pillbox')

          January   it was night
in a warehouse space   after an evening
of poetry performances
    A small warm
setting   very cold winter   (think black, red, and white)

Table set with antlers & roasted marrow

       She loud-laughing earlier at a poem
    about Vietnamese people or
I thought so   and even asked about the joke
(Did you get that on the 'inside'? I had said)

       but she being Pillbox
    said nothing and later
shared a Bic lighter by tossing it
at me—or toward me

But note   not simply 'chucking' it either
more like a side-wrist slinging

You could say she 'slung' or 'slanged' it
(the small plastic lighter)   with velocity
or maybe I could say simply   'she threw it'

    as in definitely
at me   directly   as earlier she had thrown
                    her pillbox hat
in my general direction
        though my poetry girlfriend
                    caught the hat in her lap

About the lighter   Pillbox cackled

    actually more like a smothered chortle

        She said   'Made by Dow'

That's it: 'Made by Dow'

She linking the Bic to the poem
and the line where she got it
        from my reference to napalm

in the napalm poem

        ("produced by Dow Chemical"
      said the poem)

   and so it was maybe this or the other   I don't know
which provoked the thing   her narrow laugh and throwing
the made-by-Dow lighter at me to say

   'Made by Dow'
'Made by Dow'

I since have come to say   'Made by Dow'
   and tell the Pillbox story

VIEWED FROM 2020

mother wept for not
seeing 'home' again   and then didn't

energy strand in the imagined
flower hypocrisy   (selfish)

see c. 1980 with navy thread wrapped
ornaments and shiny drunken

the fake white Xmas   small living room
'grand flight at sunset' painting

and wrong-way flying ducks   playing
directly into class traps

"dine on love's past landscapes"

\\\

turn   lost annoyance
and changing subjects

   her practiced poses
for photos

what did we know then

or now   me scoffily knowing "better"
with my Aquarius and metal placements

     look ma
       no accent

   ///

\

hinges

    more like metal-plates in the resewn
pulled-apart cloth doll

    and when asked a few sentences
to immigranty teenage angst ™

    bright regret   frayed rage and mint
    yr parents you won't ever truly know

can't get past the disruptive
drugstore surface

    fastens   you & me haughty and hungry

(x   )

when asked about the
              of the past :   the skin she quit

HEARTLESSNESS

The heartlessness of flowers
Yarrow in the dream
saying its name as I ran
the hill among flowers

   "Puts in order"
  sequential veils

Yellow yells

Past action: deadened
Present action: death wish

I wake with haunted features
and flew straight here
    inside a flower
   sail a single petal

  "which place is home/
   the road goes in circles"

I rename myself a bell to ring
having been given the dead girl's name

The dead becomes my face
the dead of my face

Plant yarrow
for your pouch to carry

WE SING TO

wing a string   we sing to
wing again

SINGS THE WISHING WELL
(THE GHOST WELL CARED-FOR)

in the story the men get to live
the wife   faithful   dies
    her death
is pious   strangled stars bangle

gather floating flowers
  underworld yourself

a beautiful dreamer
  in the mosquito myth
with visions of owning a grand house
she grows ill in the fields   dies
is arrayed in a field of flowers
  saved by blood magic she later betrays
doomed to live as nuisance
    begging begging

  don't go
again I call

newly flooded
fields of rice   farm girl sits
on the flood wall
sings the wishing well

we sing her story beyond time

wield feathers and clouds of her

a melted floating love gem

our tears mix with tears

I have no sacred rites for you
saving the sacred
grove you grew

Hùng Việt

Notes to Images

The all-women stunt motorcycle troupe that my mother belonged to was named Hùng Việt. Established in 1955, the Vĩnh Long–based group traveled to regional celebrity in southern Vietnam before disbanding in 1961 when traveling became too dangerous. One of the managers of the motorcycle troupe also owned and operated LIGHT, a photography and portrait studio in Saigon. He took some of these promotional photographs for the troupe. I do not have a record of the photographer's name.

There were five members; the names of three of the women are lost to me. In the photo where the troupe is assembled alone together, my mother is second from the left, looking directly at you. The woman on the far right is Bach Yen; she left the group after a serious motorbike fall and went on to pursue a successful international singing career.

As part of the performances, Diệp would ride to the highest mark on the barrel, the red line. She was only one of two riders who would ride hands free or in a formation on the wall. As the motorbikes circled, audience members could offer money to the riders in appreciation of their bravery, and riders would take the bills skillfully from their hands.

Her Vietnamese name was Nguyễn Anh Diệp. When she left Vietnam for North America in 1968, she became Linda Diep Lijewski. On the back of one of these photos, for the apparent purpose of giving it to someone unnamed, my mother writes as follows:

"This is a glorious time, in 1956.
In those days I was a flying motorist artist—
this is the sole memory of my life.

For my friend, to keep as a memory . . .
The flying motorist artist"

Notes to Poems

I have borrowed the descriptive phrases "clear and bell-like" and "bends towards the Vietnamese voice" from *Loa*'s episode on the đàn bầu. Thank you to segment editor Nam-An Dinh and to Jason Nguyen, the musicologist featured there, especially for the đàn bầu recording playing a cover of a popular song by the Eagles.

The final line in "Spoken through the Cracked Eye" and the quoted text in "Heartlessness" are drawn from song lyrics by Trịnh Công Sơn (February 28, 1939–April 1, 2001), the popular songwriter from Huế. From his translated lyrics, I also include variations of phrases or lines for the poems "Why This Haunted Middle . . ." and "Fortune Cookie No Fortune."

References to *Colloquial Vietnamese* correspond to the Routledge publication by Tuan Duc Vuong and John Moore, subtitled *A Complete Language Course*. Poems sourced from it are drawn from the 1994 edition that came with cassette tapes.

The italicized line in "Less Than Slash Three" is adapted from Sappho fragment 118, translated by Anne Carson.

I have re-created three Vietnam ghost stories shared on the *Saigoneer* April 13, 2018 podcast; many thanks to contributors Khoi Pham, Nguyen Thi, and Mike Tatarski for the original tellings.

The text in the poem "Scooby-Doo Villain Ghoul Method A.K.A. US Military Psychological Operation 'Wandering Soul'" is adapted translated audio of this propaganda campaign from "Ghost Tape Number 10" uploaded in 2012 to YouTube.

"'O My 4FH Planes'" is drawn from documentary footage of a folk opera performed for villagers in North Vietnam by two North Vietnamese, government-sponsored actors as recorded and translated in the French 1967 anti-war documentary collaboration *Far from Vietnam*.

For "Failed Tower Ca Dao," I am indebted to the tarot scholarship and writing of Rachel Pollack. For this poem and many others in the collection, I must thank my fellow time travelers, the often anonymous tellers of tales, diviners, singers, and makers of poetry.

Acknowledgments

The following journals originally published poems or versions of the poems presented here: Academy of American Poets Poem-a-Day, *Ambit, Arc, The Bare Life Review, Berkeley Poetry Review, boundary 2, Brooklyn Rail, carte blanche, diaCRITICS, EVENT, Jai-Alai, Poetry,* PoetryNow, *The Puritan, Saigoneer,* and *Vallum.* Some also were drawn into the anthologies *The Best Canadian Poetry in English 2015, The Best of the Best Canadian Poetry in English 2017, The Plume Anthology of Poetry 3,* and *Pushcart Prize XLIV.* Additionally, the venues Boise Free Poetry, Belladonna*, and knife | fork | book published selections and/or versions of these poems as parts of their chapbook series. I offer endless gratitude to these curators and to the organizations and readers who support these outlets: thank you.

The following organizations have provided occasions, community, and residency essential to the creation of this manuscript: the Diasporic Vietnamese Artist Network (DVAN), the Djerassi Resident Artists Program, the MacDowell Colony, the Millay Colony for the Arts, and Villa Ghjiasepina. I could not have written this book without the resources, support, and relationships I found there.

Endless thanks to generous grants from the Ontario Arts Council and the Canada Council for the Arts. They made this book possible.

I would like to extend extra gratitude to the She Who Has No Masters collaborative with special thanks to co-founder, organizer, and *diaCRITICS* editor extraordinaire Dao Strom. My thanks also go to novelist Anna Moï for translating the two-part letter from Nguyễn Lê Thị (my mother's aunt), with additional gratitude to poet and novelist Nguyễn Phan Quế Mai for her aid in translating newspaper clippings and a photo dedication.

Cascades of thanks and love to my dear friends and family far and near; you life me.

Love eternal and endless to the water signs that I am lucky to share this life with: Keaton, Waylon, and my beloved, Dale.